Art Nouveau
GLASS PAINTING

Alan Gear and
Barry Freestone

David & Charles

A DAVID & CHARLES BOOK

First published in the UK in 2003

Copyright © Alan Gear and Barry Freestone

Distributed in North America
by F&W Publications, Inc.
4700 East Galbraith Road
Cincinnati, OH 45236
1-800-289-0963

A catalogue record for this book is available from the British Library.

ISBN 0 7153 1463 7 hardback
ISBN 0 7153 1464 5 paperback (USA only)

Printed in Singapore by KHL Printing Co Pte Ltd
for David & Charles
Brunel House   Newton Abbot   Devon

Commissioning Editor   Fiona Eaton
Desk Editor   Jennifer Proverbs
Executive Art Editor   Ali Myer
Designer   Prudence Rogers
Production Controller   Jennifer Campbell

Visit our website at www.davidandcharles.co.uk

David & Charles books are available from all good bookshops; alternatively
you can contact our Orderline on (0)1626 334555 or write to us at FREEPOST
EX2 110, David & Charles Direct, Newton Abbot, TQ12 4ZZ (no stamp required
UK mainland).

contents

Introduction

Our love of glass painting, and Art Nouveau glass in particular, came about separately but via a common route. For Alan, it was picking up a book that literally changed his life. The title of the book is long forgotten, but the pictures of stained-glass windows by Louis Comfort Tiffany started a lifelong love of the colour and design that he came to know as Art Nouveau. Barry was inspired by a lamp belonging to his mother. Its intricacy and stunning colours inspired him to find out more about the designer whose work it was based on – the very same Tiffany – and he has had an abiding love of the style ever since.

The term 'Art Nouveau' comes from the Parisian shop and gallery of the same name, opened in 1895 to showcase the work of modern designers, painters and sculptors. Art Nouveau was used in every artistic form – glass, sculpture, architecture, metalwork, painting, textiles and jewellery. It was developed in the 1880s and was at its zenith during the 1890s. The essence of the style is the use of flowing lines – designs seem to grow organically rather than follow a rigid geometry. Nature, and in particular the plant world, was a great influence and is closely associated with the style. By the early years of the 20th century, Art Nouveau had begun to diminish in popularity, although its influence can still be seen today.

This book features twenty Art Nouveau-inspired glass painting projects suitable for glass painters of all abilities. If you have never tried glass painting before, the illustrated instructions will take you through the process step by step. For those who need further guidance, the beginning of the book details the techniques you will be using, while a section on materials and equipment describes some of the paints and products available and how to use them. Many of the projects have templates to help you with the design.

The projects feature clear influences of the greatest practitioners of Art Nouveau style. The works of Tiffany are the inspiration for the Dragonfly Lamp and the Plant Stand, while the distinctive style of Charles Rennie Mackintosh led to our creation of a Mosaic-Effect Mirror. As well as Art Nouveau, we have included related styles of the time, such as the works of the Arts and Crafts movement, a precursor to later Art Nouveau styles, with a William Morris-inspired Fruit Bowl. This overview of the whole Art Nouveau period has allowed us to interpret different designs in our projects.

We had so much enjoyment developing glass painting techniques that enabled us to enter the world of Art Nouveau, and we hope that you get as much pleasure as we did.

Alan & Barry

Materials and Equipment

There are many specialist materials available from craft shops, mail-order catalogues and some do-it-yourself stores which can be used to create a range of wonderful effects in glass painting. However, don't feel restricted in their application – as you gain confidence and become familiar with the materials, you will begin to discover many new ways of using them.

For comfort and safety, use your equipment on a flat, clean surface, keeping glass, paints and sharp implements beyond the reach of children. Old carrier bags, cut open and laid flat, will a give water-repellent protection to the surface underneath.

Have fun and explore the vast selection of paints, outliners and brushes available

THE BASIC KIT

These materials will form the basis of your glass painting kit. See Techniques, pages 10–13, for tips on how to use them.

Glass paints

There are many types of glass paints on the market, either solvent- or water-based, and they come in different consistencies. Thick water-based paints can be thinned with water if necessary, although some are naturally free flowing. Drying times vary and can take anything from 30 minutes to 10 days, depending on the paint you use. Some need to be baked in an oven to make them more resistant.

You don't have to use only specialist glass paints: look at other types of paint. Many will say on the label whether they are suitable for use on glass. For solvent-based paints, manufacturers will often

produce their own solutions for cleaning brushes. Water-based paint can be cleaned from brushes with soap and water. Whichever paint you choose always read the manufacturer's instructions and safety advice on the bottles.

Outliner

Outliner is used to form the basic structure of a design. Originally it was used to represent the leading in stained-glass windows, but is now used in many other ways, such as to create relief patterns. It is available in various colours but black, grey, gold and silver are the most popular. Outliners come in different containers, such as metal tubes and plastic bottles, and all have a nozzle at the end. An alternative way to apply outliner is to use an outlining bag (see Techniques, page 12). Outliner can be watered down and used as paint.

Permanent marker pens or self-adhesive lead strips can also be used to outline the design on your project – it is worth experimenting to find out which effects you prefer, and for what each one is most suitable.

Brushes

Brushes produced specifically for glass painting are readily available, however, almost any brush can be used. You may find a soft no. 2 artist's brush is most useful since soft brushes reduce brush marks in the paint – the softer the brush the fewer brush marks there will be.

For a textured effect, use a stippling brush, a piece of cut-off sponge, or a crumpled plastic bag. You can use any brush or applicator with water-based paints but solvent-based paints should only be applied with a brush.

ADDED EXTRAS

In addition to basic paint and outliner, there are various ways to add shape and colour to your glass painting projects.

Rubber stamps and foam stamps
Stamps are a very simple and effective way of transferring a pattern on to glass or acetate. Use rubber stamps to transfer detailed designs. Be sure to use an ink pad suitable for glass or acetate so that the ink won't smudge when you paint over it. Undiluted water-based glass paints can be used on less intricate rubber or foam stamps to transfer simpler designs.

Overhead projector pens
Overhead projector pens can be used on glass and acetate film and come in a range of colours. They can be a good alternative to paint when you want to apply detail in a very controlled way, such as filling in fine details or drawing an intricate design.

Paint pens
These easy-to-use pens work well on glass and film. They contain paint which is released in a controlled manner. The most popular colours are gold, silver and copper but they are also available in white, red, blue, green and black. Use them to create an outline or to add details. Porcelain pens are also available, which can be painted on glass or china and then fixed in the oven.

Permanent ink pens
Permanent ink pens are available in many colours and tip sizes. They are ideal for children to use, under careful supervision, instead of outliner. Use these pens with water-based paints, as solvent-based paints tend to dissolve the ink.

DECORATIVE TOUCHES

An ever-widening range of products are available to add further colour or textural interest to your glass painting projects, a few of which are described here.

Embellishments
Objects can be embedded in the paint for decorative effects. Tiny micro-beads can be added with glue or paint, as can beads from old costume jewellery, small shells, buttons or peel-off transfers (see page 13).

Gold leaf
Gold leaf is a fantastic addition to glass projects. You don't have to use real gold leaf – buy the cheaper Dutch metal, which comes in a range of metallic colours. Gold leaf is applied with a special glue called size. Tear the leaf into small pieces and drop into paint or attach in a sheet to the back of pre-painted projects. Protect the finished treatment with a coat of shellac.

Self-adhesive lead
This usually comes in black, platinum, silver and gold colours and in 3mm (⅛in), 6mm (¼in) and 9mm (⅜in) width strips. It is available flat or oval-shaped. Use the flat strips to bend over the edges of glass, and the oval strips flat to create a raised effect. Buy coated self-adhesive lead to prevent lead getting on your fingers as you work. See page 13 for details about using lead strip.

Get creative and experiment with all the different ways of applying colour and interest to your glass projects

**Widen your glass-painting horizons
with the endless possibilities provided
by these ingenious types of film and paper**

FILM AND PAPER

Some interesting materials have been developed to help you maximize your creative potential when working on glass projects.

Double-sided adhesive film

This handy film can be used to stick embellishments or sand to your projects. Peel away the backing sheet and stick to the glass, then peel off the top sheet and stick or sprinkle the embellishments on to it.

Thick film (500 microns)

Thick film is suitable for making cards and mobiles. The film has a protective sheet on both sides that must be removed before use.

Extra-thick film (1000 microns)

This is a good replacement for glass as it is lighter and can be cut easily into intricate shapes with a strong pair of scissors or a hot knife.

Clear self-adhesive film

This product has revolutionized glass painting. Instead of working directly on to the glass or mirror, you can outline and paint the design on to the self-adhesive film, thereby allowing you to work flat. When the design is dry, cut around it right up to the outliner, peel away the backing sheet and stick in position on the glass. Among its many other uses it can be attached to cards or decorated with embellishments such as micro-beads or fabric.

Self-adhesive copy film

This is a great film because you can photocopy any design on to it, then paint it, cut it out and stick it straight on to the glass. This type of film works best with water-based paints.

Self-cling film

This film clings to glass without the help of glue and is therefore ideal for projects that do not need to be permanent, such as window decorations – just peel away and store.

Card and paper

Use card for making aperture cards and stencils, and paper for masking off and making templates. Handmade paper and mulberry papers can be embedded into glass paint using a découpage technique.

Release paper

Outliner and paint will not stick to this coated paper, so you can paint your design on to it, leave it to dry, then peel it off. The resulting design is self-clinging and can therefore be stuck to glass without adhesive.

Self-adhesive metal

This thin silver-coloured metal can be painted, scored to make patterns, or embossed. When the backing is peeled off it can be stuck to other surfaces.

Stencils

Use pre-cut stencils or cut your own from thin card using a craft knife. Use thick, water-based paint, applied with a sponge or a stippling brush. Stencil directly on to the glass or pre-painted self-adhesive film.

TOOLS

The following are just some of the additional tools you may find handy. If they are not available, you can often improvise with every-day items.

Craft knife and scissors
A craft knife will allow you to cut complex designs precisely (always use on a cutting mat or padded surface). Use sturdy scissors to cut extra-thick film and thin metal.

Cutting mat
Use this with a craft knife when cutting stencils or card. Thick layers of newspaper or thick cardboard could also be used.

Paper trimmer
A paper trimmer is good for cutting film accurately, particularly when cutting mosaic pieces. It can also be used for creasing and cutting cards.

Hot knife
This can be used as an alternative to scissors for cutting thick and extra-thick film, especially if you want to cut very intricate designs. A hot knife is also good for cutting out small holes in film.

Hairdryer
A hairdryer is a must if you want to dry water-based paint quickly. It should not be used with solvent-based paint, however, as it will create bubbles.

Paper kitchen towel
Kitchen towel is crucial when outlining and painting. Fold it into four and keep it handy. Use to clean off any blobs of outliner on the nozzle, to clean brushes, and to dab excess paint from an overloaded brush.

Spray adhesive
Low-tack spray adhesive is useful for sticking stencils and paper masks on to glass when sponging paint.

Masking tape
Use masking tape to hold templates in place when you are tracing over them. The tape can also be used to mask out areas that you don't want to paint.

Water-based glue
This all-purpose glue is useful for a variety of techniques. Keep a pot of water handy when working with it, to wash the brush out regularly so that the glue does not dry on the bristles and ruin the brush.

Silicone glue
This handy adhesive has a tacky consistency and will hold pieces of plastic together as they dry, (see page 46). Use it to create a three-dimensional effect when building up layers of material (see page 86). Silicone glue can also be used for other general purpose tasks in your glass painting projects.

Enjoy your glass painting with a few simple but essential tools that will help you achieve professional-looking results

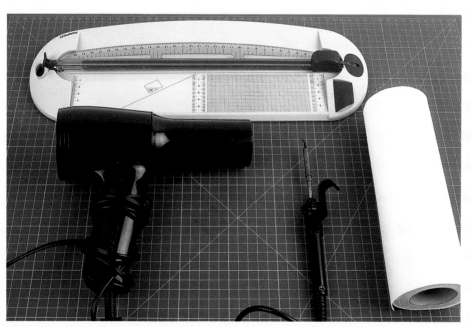

Techniques

If you are new to glass painting, there are some basic techniques you will want to try before embarking on your chosen projects. The techniques that follow are very simple and used throughout the book. Practice your skills on old glass jars, plates and tiles until you feel confident – you will probably learn a few techniques of your own as you experiment.

Once you have got to grips with the basics, experiment with different styles of application, colour and embellishment to produce your own unique and eye-catching effects. Try using glass-painting materials on surfaces other than glass, such as ceramic and plastic. If you are an artist or craftsperson, apply your own techniques to glass painting – you are sure to come up with some wonderful effects.

Working with Paint

MIXING PAINT

Diluting paint

Depending on the painting technique you want to use, you may want to alter the consistency of your paint.

Water-based paint is quite thick when it comes out of the bottle. Although there are many techniques that use it in this state, such as sponging or stippling, you can add water to alter the consistency. Mix equal parts of paint and water for a smooth, flowing consistency.

Creating colours

You can make your own colours and shades of paint by mixing them together before applying to the glass. Above, pearl white is being added to basic purple to create a pearlescent purple.

To make pastels, mix white paint with a colour – the more white you add, the paler the final colour will be. When you add white or pearl the paints will dry to an opaque finish.

Mixing on glass

Glass paints are also easy to mix on the glass itself by flicking them together with the tip of a brush. Here, blue and yellow are being mixed together to make green.

This is a useful technique to learn as it allows you to create beautiful and interesting colour effects in your projects. The Enamel-Effect Music Box (page 34) shows this technique used to stunning effect.

Adding highlights

You can add highlights to solvent-based colours by adding a blob of clear solvent-based paint to the area you have painted while it is still wet.

For water-based paint use watered-down clear paint or just water, adding a blob to the painted area while it is still wet. The Shimmering Peacock Card (page 78) uses highlights to add an extra dimension to the colours.

APPLYING PAINT

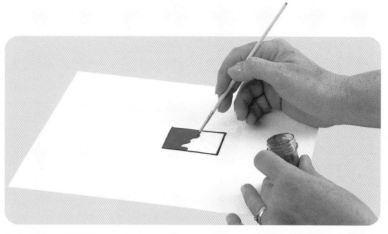

Simple brushwork

This technique is good for covering large areas of glass with an even application of paint. To achieve a smooth finish you must use a soft brush – the softer the brush, the smoother the finish will be. For the most controlled application, you will find it easiest to work either from side to side, or sweep the brush towards yourself, rather than away.

Painting details

To paint small, intricate areas, use a narrow artist's no. 2 brush. Hold the paint pot right up to the area you are painting, so that if the paint drips off the brush it is more likely to drip into the area being painted. When painting, always paint up to the edges of the outliner. It helps if you paint over a white surface and occasionally lift up the glass to see if it is touching the outliner. Let the paint dry on a smooth, flat surface to stop it from pooling on one side, and in a warm atmosphere, as moisture may affect the paint.

Sponging

Sponges come in a variety of textures and can be used to create many different effects. Dab the sponge in your paint, dab off any excess on a kitchen towel or rag, and then dab on to the glass. You can layer colours over one another, or use the sponge to apply stencils. For other textured effects try crumpled paper, old rags, toothbrushes, and even an old plastic bag.

Finger painting

Finger painting must be one of the easiest ways of applying water-based glass paints to glass or to self-adhesive film. This technique allows you to cover large areas and creates the effect of handmade stained glass. First, squeeze streaks of paint from the bottle directly on to the glass or film. Two or three colours work well. Roughly spread the paint from side to side with your finger. Do not mix the colours too much or overwork the paint with swirls or patterns as the effect will not look as good. Less is more with this technique.

Outlining and Embellishing Designs

USING OUTLINER

Outlining is a technique used to create raised lines within a design. This produces a decorative effect similar to the leading originally used in stained-glass windows. Outliners come in a range of colours in addition to black, including gold and silver. The technique requires some practise to achieve a smooth, even line, so it is worth experimenting before starting a project.

Using a bottle or tube

This method allows you to apply the outliner via the nozzle, directly from the container in which it is bought. It is easier to apply the outliner down towards you or from side to side, rather than upwards. To apply evenly, squeeze the bottle gently, lifting the nozzle ever so slightly so that the outliner is laid on to the glass or film. If you drag the tip of the nozzle along the glass you will just get a flat, uneven line. When you want to finish the line, touch the nozzle to the glass and break the line neatly.

tip

Keep the outliner bottle upside-down in a glass or a cup. This keeps the outliner at the nozzle end and ensures it is always ready to use. It also helps stop the nozzle drying out and getting blocked.

Using an outlining bag

Outliner comes in a bottle or tube with a convenient nozzle, but we prefer to use an outlining bag as it allows you to choose the thickness of line you want to use.

1

To make the bag, cut out a triangle of greaseproof or parchment paper.

2

Holding the point towards you, fold both ends into the middle to form a cone shape.

3

Fold over the ends of the cone to secure it. Half fill the cone with outliner, fold the ends into the middle and fold and roll down to seal the bag. Use scissors to cut the size hole you want in the tip.

tip

Make a fresh bag each time you run out of liner or want to use a different colour.

APPLYING SELF-ADHESIVE LEAD

Self-adhesive lead is easy to work with and can be used to separate areas of colour in a similar way to traditional stained glass. It is best to apply the lead after painting, and is easier to use it if it is at room temperature.

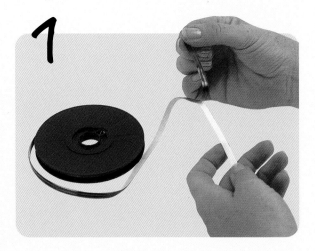

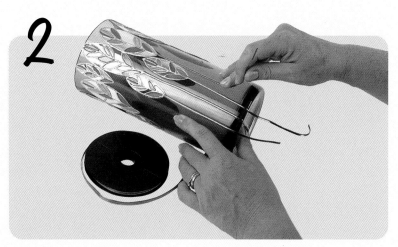

Peel away the backing paper to reveal the adhesive side of the lead, which will stick easily to glass.

Press the lead down onto the surface – using a boning tool or the shaft of a wooden tool may help, but do not use metal as it will mark the lead.

ADDING TEXTURAL DETAILS

Embedding objects into glass paint is a simple and effective way to add texture and interest to projects – try buttons, wire, shells, metal glitter, glass nuggets, sequins and beads.

Sprinkle small clear beads on to the painted area, spreading them out with the tip of a brush.

Paint over the beads to embed them into the surface. Clear beads will take on the colour of the paint. If you want to use coloured beads, apply clear paint on top.

Shimmering Stencilled Vase

Many Art Nouveau glassware designs featured lustrous, iridescent colours that reflected light like a dragonfly's wing. The most beautiful examples are by the master of Art Nouveau glass, Emile Gallé, who experimented with colour and finish to create a wealth of innovative and beautiful glassware.

The vase we have created here utilizes a shimmering background colour further enhanced by Art Nouveau-style stencils. If you can't find the Art Nouveau stencil you are looking for, cut your own design with a craft knife or stencil cutter from a sheet of stencil film or thin card. Use a stencil brush or small sponge to stencil straight on to clear glass, or on to pre-painted glass, as here. If you overlay the stencils, make sure that each layer of glass paint is completely dry first, or you may lift the paint off when you remove the stencil.

You will need
- glass vase • water-based glass paint: royal blue and purple
- gold outliner • scrap paper • stencil brush or cut-off sponge

1

Apply the royal blue and purple background paint to the vase using a soft, flat brush. Apply the paint in a thin layer, blending the colours as you go. Put to one side to dry completely.

2

Hold the stencil of your choice securely on the vase, or spray the back of the stencil with low-tack spray adhesive. Squeeze the gold outliner on to some scrap paper and using a stencil brush or small sponge off-cut, dip into the outliner, stamp off the excess and apply to the glass in quick dabbing movements. You may have to wait for the outliner to dry before moving on to the next section of the glass.

4

Complete the design with areas of interest in the middle of the vase. Here, we repeated the small diamond-shaped motif.

5

Finish off the vase with strips of self-adhesive border peel-offs along the edges. Cut the strips to length and position on the painted glass, pressing into place with a boning tool or pen if necessary.

• flat, soft paintbrush • stencil of your choice • low-tack spray adhesive (optional) • self-adhesive border peel-offs • boning tool or pen

3

Re-use the stencil in another area on the vase or use a new section of the stencil, gradually building up the design.

tip

When you want to achieve an overlayed effect, use a hairdryer to help the paint dry more quickly. This way, you won't have to wait so long for each stencilled design to dry before applying the next.

Decorative Iris Tile

Ceramic tiles were a popular way of introducing colour and design to Victorian walls, and high-relief ceramic tiles depicting natural motifs such as flowers, birds or insects in an Art Nouveau style were common as both interior and exterior decoration.

This stylized iris uses the rich colours and strong outlines typical of Art Nouveau designs. The iris was painted straight on to white tiles using glass paints suitable for tiles. Some paints can be applied to tiles *in situ* and left to dry; other paints need heating in an oven to fix the colour, so must be painted and baked before they are stuck to the wall. Check the manufacturer's instructions to make sure your paints are suitable for your intended purpose.

You will need
• plain white tiles • carbon paper • template (page 94)
• solvent-based glass paint: purple, turquoise, royal blue,

tip

If you have a number of tiles to paint, get a system established. Paint all the flowers first, then the stamens, then the stems, until the whole design is complete.

1 Clean the tiles with warm water and a little detergent and dry well. Place the carbon paper face down on the tile and place the iris template on top. You may want to tape it down so that it does not move. Trace firmly over the design with a ballpoint pen. Remove the design and carbon paper to reveal the design on the tile.

2 Begin painting the tile, blending colours as you go. Start by painting the petals in purple, turquoise, royal blue, black and white. As you blend the colours, try to create highlights and shadows. Leave the petals to dry before moving on to the next section.

4 Paint the stems in bright green, light green, yellow, black and white. Leave to dry.

5 Paint the leaves of the flowers in long, sweeping strokes in the same colours as the stems. Leave to dry.

• masking tape (optional) • ballpoint pen
black, yellow, orange, red, light green and bright green • no. 2 paintbrush

3

Paint the stamens of the flower yellow, orange and white, with a little red, blending the colours as before. Leave to dry.

Christmas Tree Bauble

The technique illustrated in this project is a very effective way of embellishing a plain glass bauble, and although the finished effect is as ornate as a Fabergé egg, it is surprisingly simple to achieve. The designs were first outlined on release paper (see page 8), which means they can be lifted off and positioned over the bauble (and repositioned until you have achieved the desired effect). The tiny pearls came from a broken necklace. Alternatively you could purchase small beads from a craft shop, or use other remnants or found objects as embellishments, such as tiny buttons or shells.

The pattern of mistletoe leaves is reminiscent of the sinuous, flowing Art Nouveau style, and the pearls call to mind René Lalique's jewellery designs. Lalique used various materials, including enamel and glass, semi-precious stones, onyx, crystal, mother of pearl, amber and ivory. They were chosen not for their value, but for their colours and surface patterns.

You will need

- glass bauble
- template (page 99)
- release paper
- water-based glass paint: light green

tip

For a pearlized effect, add a little white pearl water-based paint to the light green.

1

Place the mistletoe template under the release paper and outline the design in silver outliner.

2

Squeeze a drop of silver outliner where the mistletoe berry is to go, and carefully drop a pearl on to the outliner, using tweezers if it is easier. Gently press the pearl down into the silver outliner so that it is well embedded. Outline as many as you need and leave to dry.

5

Continue adding the mistletoe to the glass, interlacing the leaves as you go. If you are unhappy with any of the positions, peel them away from the glass and reposition.

6

Continue fitting the pieces on to the bauble until complete. It is now ready to hang.

- silver outliner • fake pearls • tweezers (optional)
- no. 2 paintbrush

3

Dilute the light green water-based paint with water to the consistency of thick cream. Fill in the leaves of the mistletoe, applying the paint generously so that when it is dry it is not too thin. Leave to dry. If it is too thin when dry, apply another coat.

4

Peel the mistletoe designs away from the release paper and, starting at the top of the bauble, lay them down on to the glass – they will self cling.

tip

Create a different colour scheme for your baubles by making bunches of red berries or gold bells using the same method as for the mistletoe.

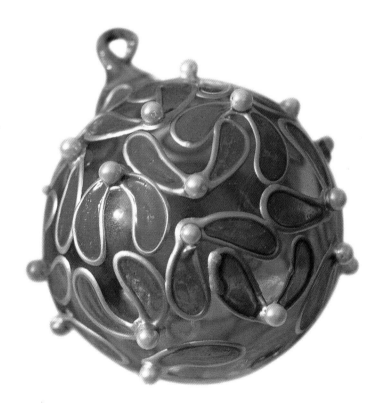

Frosted Thistle Vase

This simple, long blue vase was given an
Art Nouveau makeover by creating a thistle
design with tiny transparent beads. The
technique is a very simple and effective way
of adding pattern and texture to a plain vase.
We used clear beads on blue glass to create a
subtle effect. The beads were attached with glue
that dries clear, so the colour of the original
glass shines through. If using clear glass, you
could choose coloured beads, or clear beads
coloured with glass paints.

The stylized thistle and leaf pattern twisting up
the length of the vase, captures the spirit of
Art Nouveau design. Much of Emile Gallé's
glassware featured botanical patterns, including
leaves, grasses and flowers.

• coloured glass vase • pattern guide (page 99), • scrap paper • no. 2 paintbrush

1

The pattern is painted on to the glass freehand, so place the thistle template or design you have chosen on to the work surface as a guide. Squeeze some of the glue on to a piece of scrap paper. Dip the no. 2 brush into the glue and start painting the design from the top. Do not squeeze out too much glue at the beginning, as it will dry out. Just squeeze out a blob as you need it, and apply glue to the vase a section at a time.

2

Place the lid of a shoebox or similar on to a work surface to catch all the loose beads. Place the vase over the box lid, quite low down, so that any beads that fall are retained in the lid. Sprinkle the micro-beads liberally over the glued area.

tip

Use a hairdryer to speed up the drying time of the glue to make this project easier and quicker to complete.

4

Slowly build up the design on the glass bit by bit – allowing the glue to dry section by section makes it easier to hold the vase as you add more beads.

5

Continue the process until the vase is finished. Leave to dry thoroughly.

or design of your choice • thick, clear-drying, water-based glue • lid of a shoebox or similar • pot of small micro-beads

3

Turn the vase over and give it a few taps with your finger so the excess beads fall into the box lid. You can patch up any small areas on the glass with a dry brush or the tip of your finger. Tip all the excess beads back into the pot directly from the box lid. (Notice how few beads you have actually used.) Allow this section to dry before moving on to the next.

Iridescent Lily Card

This striking card was inspired by the work of Charles Rennie Mackintosh, who had his own distinctive interpretation of the Art Nouveau style. His elegant geometry and rendering of natural forms are shown to wonderful effect in the Glasgow School of Art and the Willow Tea Room, also in Glasgow.

The lily on this card was inspired by the Mackintosh rose design, and the two folding flaps from a less likely source – the backs of his black chairs. The lily design was imprinted into a sheet of self-adhesive metal and then painted, making the card substantial enough to be used as a picture afterwards. Alternatively, you could apply the design to thick film and insert it into an aperture card.

tip

The embossed metal makes an attractive feature in itself, so if you are short of time, leave the border details unpainted. The embossed features will still be clearly visible.

1

Lay the sheet of self-adhesive metal on to the work surface and tape the lily template over it. Trace the design with a ballpoint pen.

2

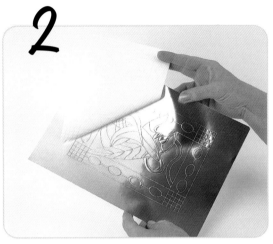

Remove the template to reveal the design indented into the metal.

5

With a ruler and pencil, mark out two rows of evenly spaced 2.5cm (1in) square on scrap paper. Using carbon paper, transfer the design to black card, positioning it on both sides of the card (see finished photograph). Cut out the squares with a craft knife and ruler on the cutting mat.

6

Crease the card so that it folds neatly. You could use a paper trimmer to do this – placing the card over the groove in the trimmer and running the blunt side of a pair of scissors along the card to produce an indentation.

- ballpoint pen • masking tape • silver outliner • no. 2 paintbrush
- black card 33 x 25.5cm (13 x 10in) • carbon paper • craft knife • cutting mat

3

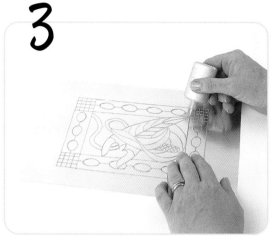

Outline the design with silver outliner, following the indentations in the metal. Leave to dry.

4

Paint in all the black sections on the card, using the finished photograph as a guide. Leave to dry, then paint all the iridescent sections on the card.

7

Peel away the backing from the self-adhesive metal and stick it to the middle of the card, then bend the card ends over into the middle.

Enamel-Effect Music Box

Beautiful enamel finishes can be seen on myriad examples of Art Nouveau jewellery and ceramics, including work by Charles Rennie Mackintosh. The design shown here was very simple to make and can be used to decorate any type of box lid. We chose a music box, but the rich enamel-like design could be used on a jewellery box or other small decorative container.

The wonderful, enamel effect was achieved by using pearlized, solvent-based paints, but other paints, such as frosted or glitter glass-paints, could be used to create different effects. Depending on the structure of your box lid, we have provided a variety of designs to choose from, but the technique is the same for all of them. You could make extra painted disks and change them from time to time, or why not create a whole set of boxes to display?

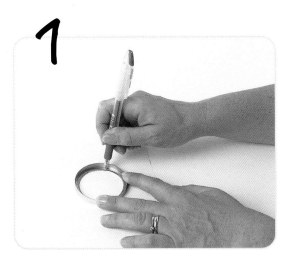

Remove the lid of the music box, place it on top of the acetate film and draw around the inside of the lid with a ballpoint pen.

Prepare the pearl paint 5 minutes before you use it. Use a flat-headed screwdriver or similar tool to stir the paint at the bottom of the jar where the pearl pigments will have settled. Replace the lid and give the bottle a good shake for 15 seconds or so. Let it rest so that the air bubbles disperse.

Choose a template from page 102 and place it under the release paper. Outline the design in gold outliner and leave to dry.

Once the painted circle is dry, cut it out with scissors, making sure you cut on the outside of the pen line so that it fits the aperture of the lid.

- flat-headed screwdriver or similar tool for stirring paint
- no. 2 paintbrush • templates (page 102) • release paper • gold outliner • scissors

3

Paint your design randomly on the acetate, in the circle and just over the line, using a mixture of brown, amber and yellow paints. You do not need to outline on the acetate – the surface tension of the paint will be enough to contain it.

4

The paint will take up to 20 minutes to dry (although overnight would be better). While drying, it will naturally mingle and create fantastic effects. To produce highlights and enliven the colour, add some white, which will blend into the colours and make it look more interesting when dry.

tip

The white pearl paint can be added at any time over the first 15 minutes. If you vary the painting times the effects will be different when dry.

7

When the outliner is dry, peel the design away from the release paper.

8

Lay the design on to the painted circle – it will cling without adhesive.

9

Place your design on the top of the music box and replace the lid. Make as many of the painted discs as you wish in different colour combinations.

Opulent Butterfly Card

Insects featured widely in Art Nouveau designs, especially in jewellery. In many ways the insect motif was ideally suited to the Art Nouveau style, as it allowed designers to incorporate rich, shimmering colour and sinuous form in pieces of breathtakingly detailed craftsmanship.

This card was worked with glass paints on thick acetate, allowing the colours to glow like jewels when caught in the light. Gold outliner was used to create the detail, echoing the intricate gold work of the best Art Nouveau jewellery designers, such as Charles Robert Ashbee and René Lalique. We like to think that Sarah Bernhardt, a leading actress of the day, would have loved to have received this card on a first night performance, since she had a passion for Lalique jewellery and often commissioned pieces for specific stage roles.

You will need • A4 (US letter) size pearlescent card • plain card, slightly
• templates (pages 98/99) • ballpoint pen • craft knife and cutting mat
• no. 2 paintbrush • solvent-based transparent glass paint: cerise, turquoise, purple,

1

Fold the A4 pearlescent card in half. Open it up and place it face down on the work surface. Lay a piece of carbon paper face down on the left-hand side of the card. Secure butterfly template A over the carbon paper with a few strips of masking tape, then carefully trace over the design with a pen. The carbon paper will transfer the design to the card.

2

Place the card on a cutting mat and carefully cut out the centres of the designs with a craft knife. Cut just outside the designs so that you don't have any black lines showing. Save all the cut-out pieces to use on other cards.

tip

Let each section dry before painting an adjoining section to keep the colours from running into each other.

5

When the gold outliner is dry, start painting the card. Here, the butterfly wings were painted purple and cerise, with some clear highlights, and the leaves were painted light green and bright green.

6

Continue painting in the details, mixing colours as you go. The flowers were painted turquoise and clear, with yellow centres. When you have finished painting, leave the card to dry completely, ideally overnight.

smaller than A4 to use as an insert • carbon paper • masking tape • acetate or thick film (500 microns), 14 x 10cm (5½ x 4in) • gold outliner clear, yellow, bright green, light green, deep aqua and amber • double-sided tape

Take the sheet of acetate or thick film and tape it on the card, just up to the fold, with double-sided tape. Check that the card folds easily.

Place butterfly template B under the card so that it shows through the holes, and trace around the design with the gold outliner. When outlining around each cut-out section keep the outline on the card side, so that when the card is finished you will not see any gaps. Leave the outliner to dry.

Once the outliner and paint is totally dry on the inside of the card, turn it over. Transfer the details of template B to the front of the card with carbon paper, or simply use it as a guide to follow by eye. Use the gold to outline as before. The film sections are easy – just follow the outlining on the other side. When the outline is completely dry, fold the card in half. Add the card insert by folding it in half and sticking into the card with double-sided tape.

Orange and Leaf Fruit Bowl

William Morris' Arts and Crafts movement revolutionized English design in the Victorian era. In an age of increasingly mechanized production, his designs were handcrafted by skilled artisans. Inspiration came from the natural world, particularly plants and birds. His textile and wallpaper patterns were often based around a repeating grid or lattice-type design, a look that was to influence many designers of the Art Nouveau period. The natural elements within Morris' patterns had a simplicity reminiscent of medieval tapestries.

This fruit bowl was inspired by one of Morris' tapestries, and incorporates the simplified repeat patterns and strong outlines characteristic of his designs. This pattern is of oranges, but the choice of design is yours. This project uses release paper, which allows you to paint the design first and then stick the component parts to the bowl, fitting them together rather like a jigsaw. Any leaves that overlap or extend beyond the rim can be trimmed with scissors.

You will need
• large glass bowl • templates (page 101) • black outliner
• water-based glass paint: orange, yellow, amber, bright green and light green

tip

To make the bowl less transparent, add pearl water-based paint to the transparent colours to produce a more opaque effect.

1

Outline the orange and leaf template on a sheet of release paper using black outliner. Fill the release paper with as many designs as you can fit on. Outline some single leaves too – these will fill in the odd blank space on the bowl. Leave the outlines to dry out completely, ideally overnight.

2

Water down the paints to the consistency of thick pouring cream. Paint the oranges, adding highlights and shading in yellow and amber, but do not use water to create highlights as this will thin the paint and make it too thin to peel away from the release paper (see tip below right).

5

When dry, the painted designs can be lifted off the release paper. Start with one corner of a design and peel it off. Place the designs on to the glass bowl, randomly fitting them closely together as you go. They will stick to the glass without adhesive. Fill in any spaces with individual leaves.

6

If at any time parts of the painted designs don't fit, trim them down with a pair of sharp scissors. The bowl is now ready to fill with fruit. The outside of the bowl should be kept dust-free with a soft cloth, and wipe the inside using a damp cloth or sponge – do not immerse in water.

3

Paint the leaves in the same way as the oranges, using bright green and light green paint. You can paint within the black outlines of the leaves if you wish, but it gives more strength to each piece if you paint over the veins of the leaves. When finished, leave to dry.

4

Repeat the black outlining over the painted leaves and leave to dry.

tip

When painting on release paper use a generous quantity of paint, otherwise it may pool and create holes,

Stamped and Gilded Box

This gilded box was inspired by the gleaming metalwork produced during the Art Nouveau era. Copper, silver, wrought iron and pewter are just a few of the metals transformed into stylish objects such as cutlery, tea sets, jewellery boxes, figurines and home accessories.

Rubber stamping is a great way to incorporate designs on to all kinds of different materials, and works wonderfully on glass. There is a wide variety of Art Nouveau stamp designs available – why not see what is on the market and let the design your choose inspire your project? The stamp design used here suggested an octagonal-shaped box. Your own stamp design might suggest a different shape – it is simple to reduce the number of sides. The design was coloured with overhead projection pens, but of course glass paints could be used instead. Gold leaf was used to finish off the box, making it gleam like lacquerware.

You will need
• rubber stamp with border • gold paint pen • scissors • size • no.2 paintbrush • gold leaf • black waterproof ink pad

tip

Use firm and even pressure when applying the rubber stamp to the film, then lift it off carefully, holding the film as you do so to avoid smudging the ink.

1

Ink the stamp using the waterproof ink pad then stamp the design on to the extra-thick film. Use the space wisely so that you stamp as many designs as required. This box is eight-sided, but you could make more or fewer sides.

2

When the ink is dry, start to fill in the colours with the overhead projection pens. Work with one colour at a time, starting at the centre and leaving each colour to dry before adding the next. Take care that the colours don't smudge into one another.

5

Protect the gold leaf with a coat of shellac and leave to dry. Lay the pieces together, face down on the work surface. Apply a bead of silicone glue along the joins and leave to dry. The glue will be touch dry within an hour and completely dry if left overnight.

6

All the pieces of the film will now be joined together. If there are any weak points apply some more glue and leave to dry.

- extra-thick, rigid film (1000 microns) • overhead projector pens in various colours
- soft-bristled brush • shellac • shellac brush • silicone glue • ruler • gold outliner

3

Use the gold paint pen to fill in the border of the design. Repeat for the remaining designs. Leave the paint to dry, then use scissors to cut the designs out of the film.

4

Turn over each design and apply a thin coat of size to the back. Leave this for about 15 minutes to allow it to become tacky. Lay the gold leaf over the top and pat it down with a soft brush. Pull off the excess leaf, reserving it for another project.

7

Measure and make a base out of rigid film to fit the bottom of the box, so that the sides either sit on top of it, or fit around the edges. Apply size and gold leaf as before. Glue the sides to the base and leave to dry.

8

Finish the box with an edging of gold outliner around the top and down the sides.

Peacock Feather Tank

The peacock featured in many Art Nouveau designs, from James MacNeil Whistler's Peacock Room, with its gold painted peacocks on the window shutters and rich peacock-blue walls, to the jewellery of Charles Robert Ashbee. We have used the peacock as inspiration for several projects in this book. The effect achieved here echoes the lustrous peacock patterns of Tiffany's fantastic iridescent *favrile* glass.

The design for this tank uses real peacock feathers, producing an authenic Art Nouveau feel. The feathers are applied to self-adhesive film using water-based paint, and embellished with a gold pen and pieces of gold leaf. We've used a straight-sided tank as it is easier to apply the feathers and film to a straight, flat surface.

You will need
• flat paintbrush • peacock feathers • water-based paint: clear and iridescent • straight-sided glass tank • gold paint pen • gold leaf

1

2

With a flat, soft brush, apply a thin layer of clear water-based paint over the self-adhesive film. While the paint is still wet, lay the feathers carefully on top and fan them out. Gently press the feathers down with the palm of your hand. Do not put any more paint on top yet – let the underside dry first so that the feathers stick to it and don't move when you apply the other layers of paint.

When the paint has dried and the feathers are securely stuck to the film, brush another thin layer of clear paint over the feathers. Then, before it dries, lay some scraps of gold leaf randomly on to the feathers. Take the flat brush and, with a little paint, brush over the gold leaf to secure it. Leave to dry, or speed up the process with a hairdryer.

5

6

When the sheets of film are dry, cut them to size. Peel away the backing from the first sheet and stick to one side of the glass tank, making sure there are no air bubbles underneath. If you don't get the position right, peel it off carefully and reposition. Repeat for all four sides.

Finish off the vase with strips of self-adhesive lead around the top, bottom and corners, pressing the strips firmly so that they stick well (see page 13).

- sheets of clear self-adhesive film, enough to cover the sides of the tank
- self-adhesive lead strips, 3mm (⅛in) wide

3

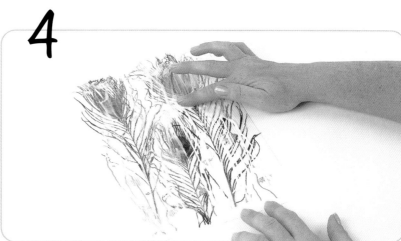

4

When dry, use the gold paint pen to doodle random gold lines down the film. Leave to dry.

Squeeze clear paint and a small amount of iridescent paint on to the film and finger paint from top to bottom (see page 11). Place somewhere warm and leave to dry out completely, ideally overnight.

tip

You can use any type of feather with this technique – many craft and home stores have a selection of both natural and pre-dyed feathers. If using feathers you have found outdoors, ensure they are clean and dry before you begin.

Mosaic-Effect Mirror

Trees were a recurring theme with many Art Nouveau designers and Charles Rennie Mackintosh was no exception, featuring them in his watercolours, furniture designs and, in particular, the Willow Tea Rooms in Glasgow. This design was inspired by the stylized tree on a mahogany washstand.

The geometric mosaic-effect works well on this modern mirror, and was created by painting sheets of copy film that were then cut into small mosaic squares – just follow the grid pattern to create the design. If the mirror is to be used in a bathroom, you could make matching accessories based on the same design, such as a toothbrush holder, soap dish or bottles of eau de toilette.

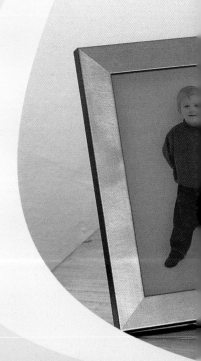

You will need

- template (page 94) • paper trimmer • mirror (portrait shaped) • scissors • self-adhesive copy film • self-adhesive clear film • clear tape

tip

When sticking the squares in place, you can either follow the design from the main photograph, or colour in the template with coloured pencils to use as a guide.

1

Finger paint on to the copy film (see page 11). Use one colour per sheet or paint half a sheet in one colour and the other half in another. We used royal blue, turquoise, cerise, black and white pearl. Enlarge the template to fit the width of your mirror – this will tell you how big the mosaic squares will be. Cut the film sheets up into squares of this size.

2

Place the template underneath the self-adhesive clear film, taping it down, so it does not move as you work. Now peel the backing paper away from the coloured squares and stick them down on to the clear film, following the pattern and colour scheme on the main photograph.

5

Peel away the backing sheet from the design. Lay the design on the mirror, ensuring there are no creases in the film, and press down gently. Use the bottom strip of the template as a guide to make a cerise and white pearl strip long enough to run down the centre of the mirror.

6

Starting with the 3mm (⅛in) self-adhesive lead, cut strips a little longer than the area you want to cover – this helps to position the lead over the design. Peel away the backing paper from the lead and stick it to the mirror, repositioning it if necessary.

- water-based glass paint: royal blue, turquoise, cerise, black and white pearl
- self-adhesive lead strips, 3mm (⅛in) and 6mm (¼in) wide • boning tool • craft knife

3

Continue adding the squares of painted film to the clear film, building up the design as you go.

4

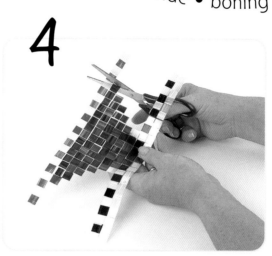

When the design is complete use a pair of scissors to cut away all excess film around the design.

7

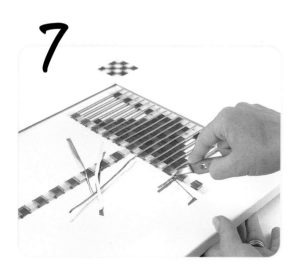

When all the lead is laid in one direction, press it down with a boning tool or the end of a plastic pen. Cut away any excess and overlapping lead with a craft knife.

8

Repeat the process, positioning the lead going the other way across the mirror. When you have finished, use a boning tool to rub over the lead to press it down firmly on to the mirror, pressing really well at the joins. Decorate the mirror frame in the same way.

tip

Always work in one direction with the lead. In this case, the lead was worked from the top to the bottom of the project, then from side to side.

Metallic Leaded Vase

The combination of metal and glass was used to great effect in many areas of Art Nouveau, including jewellery and glassware. The long, slim design of this vase has echoes of Charles Rennie Mackintosh in its stylized natural forms and geometrical precision.

When working with coloured glass, choose strong shades that won't be overwhelmed by the base colour. Add white or pearl to the glass paints to make them more opaque and the colour stronger. This project uses metal-coloured paint pens rather than glass paint, applied to self-adhesive metal. Strips of self-adhesive lead create the undulating lines so characteristic of the Art Nouveau style.

1

Trace the different sized leaf templates from page 103, cut them out and carefully tape them down on to the self-adhesive metal.

2

Trace over the templates with a pen so that the design is imprinted into the metal underneath. Do not press too hard – just enough so that the outline is clearly visible.

tip

When peeling the paper backing from the metal, place the metal face down on the work surface and peel the paper towards you to prevent the metal from curling.

5

Cut out the leaves with a pair of scissors, trimming as closely as possible to the outliner but taking care not to snip through it. Peel the paper backing away from the leaves.

6

Stick the leaves all the way round the top of the glass, varying the sizes of the leaves as you go. Start by sticking the larger leaves around the glass, and use the smaller sizes to fill the gaps in between.

- self-adhesive metal • masking tape • ballpoint pen
- self-adhesive lead strips, 3mm (⅛in) wide

3

Following the imprinted design, outline in silver and leave to dry. Work from left to right (or right to left if you are left handed), and from top to bottom. This will help avoid smudging the sections you have just outlined. Leave the outliner to dry thoroughly.

4

Use the gold and copper metallic pens to fill in the outlined sections. Leave some sections of the design blank so that the metal foil shines through, giving a third metallic colour. Leave to dry.

tip

If you don't have any self-adhesive metal, use thin metal sheets to make the leaves and use spray glue to stick them on to the glass.

7

Use the self-adhesive lead to create stems trailing down from the leaves. Press the lead down well so that it sticks firmly to the glass (see page 13).

8

Now wrap long strips of self-adhesive lead around the vase to create wavy outlines. Press down on to the glass so that the lead sticks well. Stick a strip of lead around the top and base of the glass to finish.

Filigree Candlestick

Traditionally, objects created during the Art Nouveau period were prized more for their artistic qualities than for their functional design. In Emile Gallé's glassware, for instance, feeling or sensation was more important than practical purpose, and his sensuous designs became increasingly elaborate during his career.

This striking candlestick was designed to be both decorative and multi-functional. If you remove the top decoration and turn it over, it could be used as a dish for nuts, chocolates or even ice cream. The body of the candlestick is coloured with water-based paint and decorated with a filigree pattern in silver outliner. The top section is made from thick film, painted and outlined in silver.

You will need

- no. 2 paintbrush
- thick film (500 microns)
- scissors or hot knife
- templates (page 100)
- ruler
- flat-headed screwdriver

1

Enlarge the main candle template on page 100 to the size you require. Place the thick film over the template and outline in silver outliner. Put to one side and leave to dry.

2

Dilute the paints with equal parts of water to make them flow more easily, and paint the flowers in royal blue and purple, with blobs of water to create highlights.

tip

Do not score the film with anything sharp, such as a craft knife, as it will cause the film to break when you bend it.

5

The film has to be scored before folding. Place a ruler across the film where you want it to fold. Using a blunt corner of a screwdriver, score once across the back of the painted film. Fold the film along the score line for a neat, straight, fold. You can bend the film both ways and it will not snap.

6

Fold the design into any permutation you wish – flowers up, flowers down, or a combination of the two. Slip over the candlestick once folded.

• silver outliner • water-based glass paint: royal blue, purple, clear, bright green, silver and yellow
• glass candlestick • masking tape • flat, soft paintbrush • release paper

3

Paint the leaves in bright green and light green and leave to dry. Paint the body of the design in silver, then add the yellow details. Leave the paint to dry, ideally overnight.

4

When the design is thoroughly dry, cut it out with sturdy scissors or a hot knife (a hot knife is easier). Cut up to the outline, but be careful not to cut into it. If you are using a hot knife, be especially careful not to touch the outliner with the knife. As the unpainted plastic is clear, a little left around the cut-out design will not show. Cut out the centre with scissors or a hot knife.

7

Cover the edges and top of the candlestick with masking tape. Apply royal blue and purple paint with a flat, soft paintbrush, painting the strokes evenly up and down the glass, blending the colours as you go. Peel off the masking tape and tidy up any paint with a craft knife. Leave to dry completely.

8

Using the template, outline the filigree designs on release paper and leave to dry overnight. Peel the designs off and place on to the stem of the candlestick. They will cling without adhesive. Place the top over the candlestick and insert a candle, or use the candlestick upside-down as a container for nuts, chocolates and other nibbles.

warning!

Never leave candles unattended and do not let the candle burn right down to the wick.

Gilded Glass Picture Frame

This picture frame design was inspired by many sources: the composition echoing the style of William Morris, yet the fluidity of the lines connecting it with some of the more extravagant decorative elements of Art Nouveau. Gold leaf was added to the back of the painted glass to create a rich, glowing quality reminiscent of the works of Gustav Klimt. The use of a female figure in an abstract, decorative setting recurred throughout the Art Nouveau period, as seen in works by artists such as Alphonse Mucha, Aubrey Beardsley, Sir Alfred Gilbert, and Klimt.

The design was painted on to a simple clip frame with solvent-based paints. Black outliner was used to re-create the effect of leading. We have used gold leaf, as the colour complements those we have chosen for the design, but other metal leaf could be used depending on your chosen colour scheme.

You will need

• clip frame • template (page 100) • black outliner • no. 2 paintbrush • soft paintbrush • size

1

Enlarge the template to fit the size of your clip frame. Remove the glass from the frame and lay it over the template. Trace the lines with black outliner, including the edges of the glass. Leave to dry.

2

Begin painting, following the finished photograph as a guide for the colours. Paint the dress with cerise and purple, adding clear highlights. Fill in the flowers in red, again adding clear highlights.

tip

Apply the size in a thin, even layer to avoid excess lumps and creases in the thin gold leaf. Don't worry about the gilded areas not drying perfectly flat – any texture will add to the opulent effect.

5

Turn the glass over and brush size around the painted border only – not over the centre, which is for the photo. Leave the size to dry for about 15 minutes, or until tacky.

6

Lay sheets of gold metal leaf over the sized area, allowing the sheets to overlap slightly.

- solvent-based transparent glass paint: cerise, purple, clear, red, light green, peach and black
- gold metal leaf • shellac • shellac brush

3

Use light green and clear for the leaves and stems, and peach and clear for the face.

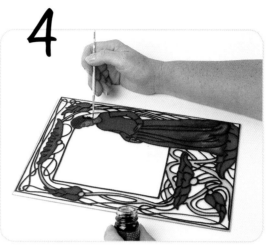

4

Paint the hair black, then leave the picture to dry completely, ideally overnight.

7

Gently press the metal down on to the glass with a soft brush. Lay off-cuts of gold leaf over any areas you may have missed and brush the metal on to the size to fill the gaps.

8

Pull off any excess metal and save it to use on other projects, then carefully paint over the metal with shellac to protect it. When completely dry place your photo in the frame and lay the glass over the top and carefully clip in place.

tip

Take care not to damage the finished design with the clips on the frame. Gently ease the clips wider before you fasten them.

Stylized Lily Storm Vase

In this project, a clear glass storm vase was transformed into a rich, colourful Art Nouveau-style piece using a variety of techniques. Once again, the design was inspired by the natural designs beloved by Art Nouveau artists. The big, bold lilies and long, slender leaves complement the strong shape of the vase, and are reminiscent of the *belle époque*, a period of prosperity in France at the end of the 19th century.

We used a finger painting technique to apply pearlescent colours to adhesive film. When dry, the colours take on the irregular appearance of antique glass. The leaves and lilies were then cut from the film and positioned around the glass with gold outliner and gold sponging adding to the shimmering, translucent effect. Fill the finished vase with cut flowers, or place a large white candle inside to highlight the colours of the glass.

- clear self-adhesive film • water-based glass paint:
- templates (page 101) • gold outliner • scissors or craft knife

tip

When finger painting, do not overdo the mixing or create too many swirling patterns. The final result should be a subtly blended effect.

Lay the sheet of clear self-adhesive film right-side up on the work surface. Apply the gold, clear and white pearl paint to the film, then finger paint from side to side. Leave in a cool place to dry. On a separate sheet of clear film, repeat the process with light green and bright green paint.

Place the gold-painted film over the lily template and outline in gold outliner. Leave to dry. This vase used four lilies; you may need more or less depending on the size of your vase. Place the green-painted film over the leaf templates, outline with gold outliner and leave to dry.

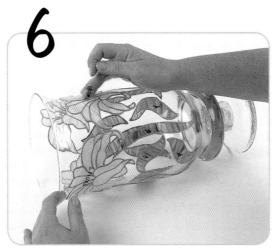

Cut out the leaf shapes, peel off the backing sheets, and stick to the glass as for the lily heads. Reserve the backing sheets as before.

Take the reserved backing sheets and place back over the design to determine which is the right way around. Then lay each backing sheet face-down on to newspaper and apply a fine spray of low-tack glue. Place each shape back over the relevant painted design to form a mask.

Using a fine sponge, apply clear and royal blue paint on the lower section of the glass. Next, sponge clear and turquoise paint to the middle section of the glass, letting it blend into the royal blue.

gold, clear, white pearl, light green, bright green, purple, turquoise and royal blue • cutting mat • glass storm vase • low-tack spray glue • newspaper • fine sponge

When dry, carefully cut out the lily shapes with a pair of scissors or a craft knife right up to the edge of the outliner.

Peel away the backing sheets to reveal the self-adhesive film. Keep the backing sheets to one side for masking (see step 6) and carefully lay each lily on to the glass vase, pressing it firmly on the glass and making sure there are no air bubbles underneath.

Sponge purple and clear paint on the top section of the glass and blend it into the turquoise.

Peel away the backing film from the designs to reveal the lily heads and leaves. Any paint that has bled on to the designs can be removed with a wet paintbrush.

Sponge gold outliner on the top and bottom of the vase. Finally, add the stamens and stems of the flowers with gold outliner. Leave to dry completely before using.

Silver-Embellished Bottle

The wide range and versatility of metals available at the beginning of the 20th century meant that almost every Art Nouveau designer turned their hand to metal work at some stage. Metals, including gold and silver, were often combined with materials such as ivory, wood, enamel and glass, to stunning effect.

In this project, we used beautiful blue bottles, that originally contained mineral water, and gave them a fine latticework of silver outliner to recreate the look of detailed silverwork. However, any straight-sided glass bottle would be suitable – try green wine bottles embellished with gold outliner for a more festive look. Fill the finished bottle with scented bath oil, or pop a candle into the top for an unusual candlestick (do not leave a candle unattended). Group several together as a focal point on the dining table.

You will need

- straight-sided blue bottle
- templates (page 95)
- scissors
- release paper
- spray adhesive (optional)

tip

It is a good idea to check that you have enough material to complete a project before you begin. In this case, a lot of outliner is required, and it would be very frustrating to run out halfway through!

1 Place the release paper over the template for the bottle and bottle neck, and tape in place to keep it flat.

2 Outline the design using silver outliner. Since you will be painting only a small part of the design, keep the outline fairly bold to give impact and strength. When finished leave to dry.

4 Carefully peel the design from the release paper. We find it easier to place the design face down on the work surface and peel the release paper from the design. Leave the design to relax back into shape for a few minutes.

5 Position the bottle on to the back of the outline design and roll it up. Any excess pieces of outliner can be trimmed with scissors. Decorate the neck of the bottle in the same way. If you want to display the cork, decorate it with a silver metallic pen.

- masking tape • silver outliner
- silver metallic pen (optional)

3

Place a little outliner in a small pot and dilute with a little water to make a more flowing consistency for painting (see tip, right). Use this to fill in the areas you wish to paint. Keep the paint plentiful on the release paper as it will tend to pool in the middle if you use too little. Leave to dry completely overnight.

tip

When watering down the outliner try to keep the consistency quite thick. If it is too thin it will tear when you come to peel it away from the release paper. You might want to practice getting this right before you start the project.

tip

The outliner can be removed from the glass by unpeeling it gently. If you want the pattern to stick permanently, spray the back with adhesive before you roll it round the bottle.

Shimmering Peacock Card

The peacock was a favourite motif for many artists throughout the Art Nouveau period and appeared in many guises and media. Louis Comfort Tiffany featured peacocks in beautiful stained-glass windows, plates and vases, while August Delaherche used the peacock feather as inspiration for the patterns on his fantastic ceramic vases. The peacock also appeared in Art Nouveau jewellery, notably in Charles Robert Ashbee's brooch designs in silver, opal and mother-of-pearl.

We, too, were inspired by the peacock, and this unusual card was made from one sheet of thick film, displaying toning shades of blue and purple highlighted with silver outliner. A message can be written on the inside of the card using a waterproof, permanent marker pen.

You will need

- water-based glass paint: yellow, black, royal blue, purple, turquoise and clear
- sheet of A4 (US letter) thick film (500 microns thick)

tip

When you buy thick film, it may have a protective film on it to prevent it from being scratched. Remove this at least one hour before you start the project, as static is created when the films are separated, and this can distort the outliner.

1

The design covers the whole sheet of film, which is folded in half when complete. When the film is ready to use (see tip, left), secure it over the template and trace over the design using silver outliner, taking care not to smudge it as you work. Leave to dry.

2

The water-based paint is a concentrate, so add a little water to achieve a flowing consistency so that it will dry flat. First, paint in all the yellow sections on the design. Then add a blob of water to the painted areas to create highlights when dry.

5

Cut around the card with a pair of sharp scissors or a hot knife. Cutting up to the silver outliner, taking care not to cut through it.

6

Paint the clear glue over the peacock, taking care not to touch the outliner. (The glue is white when wet but will dry clear.) Work on small areas at a time, so that the glue does not dry before you are ready to add the glass beads.

- silver outliner • template (page 96) • masking tape • ruler • flat-headed screwdriver
- no. 2 paintbrush • sharp scissors or hot knife • clear glue • box lid • pot of micro-beads

3

Mix a little black with the royal blue to create a darker shade, then paint in the dark blue, royal blue and purple areas of the design. Add blobs of water for the highlights as before.

4

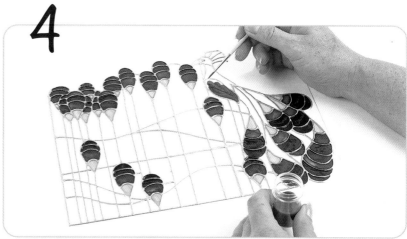

Paint the body of the peacock next, mixing the turquoise, royal blue and purple as you go. Swirl the colours together in one direction and add blobs of water for highlights. Next, paint in all the turquoise sections of the design. Finally, paint the water at the bottom of the card in royal blue and turquoise, with blobs of water added for highlights. Leave the paint to dry, then brush clear paint on to all the remaining spaces. Allow to dry completely.

7

Place the card into the box lid and sprinkle the glass beads on top of the wet glue. Gently press down on the beads, then pick up the card and knock off the excess beads. Repeat until you have beaded all the desired areas, then leave the glue to dry completely.

8

To bend the film, turn the card over and lay a ruler down the middle. With the corner tip of a flat-headed screwdriver, score down the back of the film. Do not use anything sharp like a craft knife, as this will cause the film to snap rather than bend. When you have scored the film, turn it over and bend in half to make the card.

Tiffany-Style Plant Stand

For the stained-glass artist or glass painter, Louis Comfort Tiffany stands head and shoulders above any designer. He produced some of the most stunning examples of stained glass of the Art Nouveau period, from huge-scale window panels to lampshades, and his work is highly sought after today.

This piece was inspired by Tiffany's style and use of colour. Here, we have made it to fit a plant stand, but the design could be easily adapted to fit a window, cupboard door, front door panes, or even a mirror. This is a surprisingly simple design to complete, because it is easier to outline small sections of an intricate design, as this one is, than it is to make long, sweeping outlines. Work on the pieces section by section, rather like putting together a jigsaw. You'll be amazed at the results.

You will need

- sheet of glass, cut to size • template (page 97)
- water-based glass paint: white pearl, yellow, purple,

tip

When having the glass cut, ask the glazier to take the sharp edges off to avoid cutting yourself when handling the pane.

1

Enlarge the template design to the required size, joining the two pieces together. Place the glass over the top of the design and fix in place with masking tape. Working in small sections, outline the design in black outliner, following the template. Leave to dry completely, ideally overnight.

2

If necessary, dilute the paint with a little water to achieve a flowing consistency. Start painting the first colour – in this case we used white pearl with a little yellow to create a streaky look.

4

Paint the bottom flowers in purple, turquoise and yellow, with drops of water added for highlights. Paint the leaves using deep aqua, with streaks of water to produce highlights. Leave the deep aqua paint to dry.

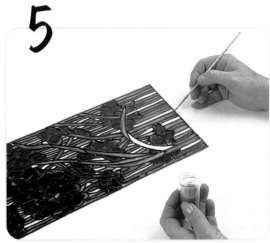

5

Now paint the remaining leaves alternately in bright green and light green, leaving the paint to dry between colours. Complete the panel by painting the top flowers royal blue and purple, with water highlights, and the branches in brown and amber. Leave all the paint to dry.

masking tape • black outliner • no. 2 paintbrush
turquoise, deep aqua, bright green, light green, royal blue, brown and amber

3

Next, paint the turquoise sections. To add highlights, add a drop or two of water on to the paint before it dries.

6

Fill in the blank areas with clear paint, swirling it thinly on the glass directly from the bottle. Do this roughly to create a textured effect when dry. Leave the whole pane to dry, and when ready fit the glass pane into the planter.

tip

If you are making a window or door pane protect the painted surfaces by laying another piece of glass over the top and sealing the edges with a bead of silicone glue and some tape. Make sure the paint is completely dry, otherwise condensation may form on the inside of the glass.

Arts and Crafts Sun Catcher

This window hanging was inspired by the designs of William Morris, and draws on his use of pattern and colour to make up the design. Morris' Arts and Crafts movement was, in part, a reaction against the increasing mechanization of the production processes of his day, and his workshop created beautiful handmade pieces, including furniture, textiles and wallpaper. His controlled patterns and natural motifs were to influence later Art Nouveau artists.

The fine detail of this design was too intricate to be cut from glass, so we made the window hanging from extra-thick film. This also makes it lighter to hang in the window, but still catches and diffuses the light beautifully. The overlayed pieces give a rich, three-dimensional effect.

You will need

- no. 2 paintbrush
- water-based glass paint: gold, royal blue, purple and red
- sheet of extra-thick film (1000 microns)

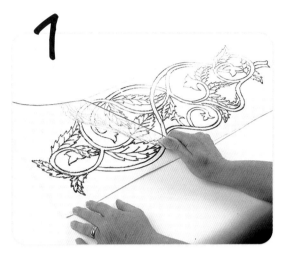

1

Enlarge the templates on a photocopier to the size you require. With sturdy scissors, cut a length of film slightly larger than the main design and place over the top, fixing in place with masking tape.

2

Outline the whole design in gold outliner, making sure the lines are big and bold and not too thin. When finished let it dry for a few hours.

tip

When going over the design with the gold outliner, don't worry about creating small blobs and bumps. This design is about creating a textured, three-dimensional effect, and any raised gold outliner will only add to this.

5

With the gold outliner, go back over the veins of the leaves to emphasize the relief and add any highlights to the swirling sections of the designs. Leave to dry.

6

Outline and paint the extra leaves in the same way as the main section of the design. Paint the roses red, then leave to dry. With the template underneath the roses, use outliner to create the relief patterns, such as the stamen and highlights.

- templates (page 103) • strong scissors • masking tape • gold outliner
- hot knife (optional) • silicone glue • bradawl (optional) • gold thread or ribbon

3

Water down the gold paint to a flowing consistency and use it to paint the whole structure of the design, going over the veins of the leaves and all details. Leave to dry.

4

Start filling in the centre section of the design with royal blue and purple paint, watered down to a flowing consistency. Blend and streak the two colours together as you go. Before the paint has dried, add blobs of water for highlights and then leave to dry completely

7

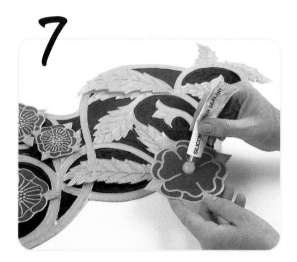

Cut out all the designs with sturdy scissors or a hot knife. Squeeze a big blob of silicone glue on to the backs of the roses and leaves.

8

Position the roses and leaves on to the larger design but do not push them down – leave them raised to create a more three-dimensional effect. Position some of the leaves slightly off-centre to help the illusion. To hang up the piece, make two holes at the top of the project with a bradawl or a hot knife and thread some gold thread or ribbon through. Tie a knot and hang in a window or on a wall.

Dragonfly Lampshade

Thomas Edison's invention of the electric light bulb in 1879 led to a huge market for electric lamps, and Louis Comfort Tiffany was one of the first to see the potential of combining electric light with coloured glass shades, resulting in a series of stunning Art Nouveau lamps. His leaded glass shades were combined with cast bronze bases and featured stylized motifs such as dragonflies or wisteria.

This lampshade uses Tiffany's dragonfly design as its inspiration, and although the effect is distinctly Art Nouveau, the technique is anything but. We have re-created the look of stained glass by painting the motifs on to clear film, which means that the designs can be painted on a flat surface first, and then positioned on the shade after they are dry. We have chosen a very modern lampshade, the simplicity of which works well with the intricacy of the surface pattern.

You will need

- water-based paint: turquoise, light green, royal blue, deep aqua, yellow, clear, amber
- lamp with glass shade
- templates (page 98)

templates (page 98)

tip

An opaque glass lampshade will give a rich, more authentic finish to your project than a clear one.

First make the dragonflies for the lampshade. The number you make will depend on the size of the lamp – this shade used six. Place the dragonfly template under the thick film, outline the dragonflies in black outliner and leave to dry. Glue on the crystal bead eyes with water-based glue and leave to dry.

Water down the paints to a flowing consistency and paint the wings in turquoise and light green and the body in royal blue and deep aqua. Add blobs of water to give highlights.

tip

Place the shade on top of something solid and stable (a vase was used here) while you are working on it.

Make the ovals in the same way as the dragonflies. Place the templates under the self-adhesive film and outline in black. When dry, paint some ovals in yellow, light green and clear and others in amber, yellow and clear. When dry, cut them out, peel off the backing and stick randomly to the shade.

With the black outliner, outline the rest of the lampshade in a random mosaic effect. Leave to dry completely.

• thick film (500 microns) • black outliner • and brown • no. 2 paintbrush • scissors • crystal beads (for eyes) • water-based glue • silicone glue • self-adhesive clear film • large paper clips

3

When the film is dry cut out the dragonflies. Spread some silicone glue over the back of the dragonflies with the tip of your finger, making sure the backs are completely covered. Lay the dragonflies around the glass lampshade, pressing them down so they stick to it. You may need to hold them in place with large paper clips to stop them lifting up while they dry. Place the shade to one side to dry.

6

When the outliner is dry start painting the body of the shade, using royal blue, turquoise, clear, deep aqua, amber and brown. Load the brush with royal blue and deep aqua and, starting at the top of the shade, twist the brush to swirl the paint down on the glass. Paint section by section, blending the colours as you go. This will create a marbled, handmade glass effect as the paint dries. Leave the shade to dry for a few days before assembling it on the lamp base.

Templates

Re-size to your requirements, unless otherwise stated.

Decorative
Iris Tile
(page 18)

Silver-
Embellished
Bottle – neck
(page 74)
Use at size shown

Mosaic-
Effect
Mirror
(page 54)

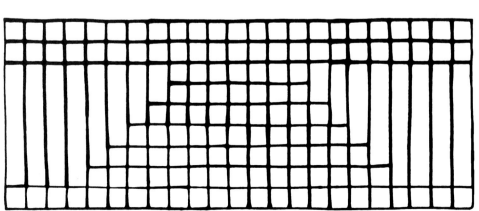

Silver-Embellished Bottle (page 74)
Use at size shown

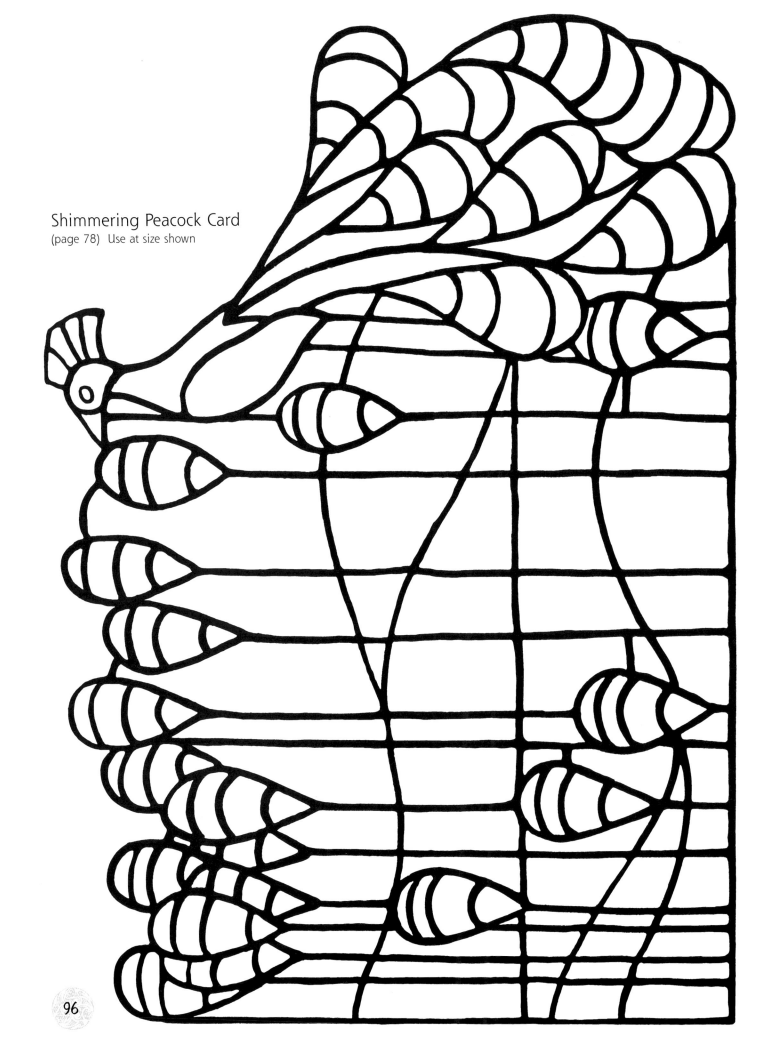

Shimmering Peacock Card
(page 78) Use at size shown

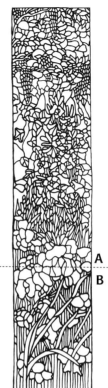

Tiffany-Style Plant Stand
(page 82)

Enlarge sections A and B to the required size. Join the two sections together (see left) to make the complete template from which you can trace the outline.

Opulent
Butterfly Card
template A
(page 38)

Use at size shown

Dragonfly
Lampshade
(page 90)

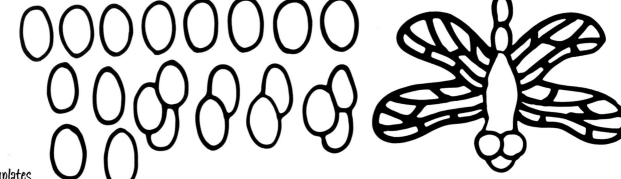

Opulent
Butterfly Card
template B
(page 38)
Use at size shown

Frosted
Thistle Vase
*Use as a guide for
freehand drawing*
(page 26)

Christmas Tree Bauble (page 22)

Gilded Glass Picture Frame (page 66)

Filigree
Candlestick
(page 62)

Lily Storm Vase
(page 70)

Orange and Leaf
Fruit Bowl
(page 42)

Enamel-Effect Music Box (page 34)

Iridescent Lily Card (page 30) Use at size shown

Arts and Crafts
Sun Catcher
(page 86)

Metallic
Leaded
Vase
(page 58)

Suppliers

The Alexander Collections
tel: 01494 434234 for nearest stockist
email: sales@alexandercollections.co.uk
Reuge music boxes

Crystal Colours
tel: 01924 275566 for nearest stockist
micro-beads and glass beads

Ideal World Television
Newark Road
Peterborough
PE1 5WG
tel: 08700 700800
www.idealworldtv.co.uk
*Also see Digital Satellite 635
and NTL 855
craft supplies*

IKEA Ltd
255 North Circular Road
London
NW10 0JQ
tel: 020 8208 5600
glassware and mirrors

L J Gibbs & Partners Ltd
Mulberry House
Hewitts Road
Chelsfield
Nr Orpington, Kent
BR6 7QS
tel: 01959 533663
email: info@ljgibbsandpartners.com
www.ljgibbsandpartners.com
handmade papers

Rainbow Glass
85 Walkden Road
Worsley, Manchester
M28 7BQ
tel: 0161 790 3025
fax: 0161 661 5787
email: sales@rainbowglass.co.uk
www.rainbowglass.co.uk
*water-based and solvent-based
glass paints, glass painting films,
self-adhesive lead and other glass
painting equipment*

Staedtler (UK) Ltd
Pontyclun
Mid Glamorgan
Wales
CF72 8YJ
tel: 01443 237421
email: marketinguk@staedtler.com
www.staedtler-uk.co.uk
metal leaf

West Designs
Unit 1a Park Farm Road
Folkestone, Kent
CT19 5EY
tel: 01303 247110
email: sales@westdesign.cix.co.uk
www.westdesignproducts.co.uk
*paper trimmers, rotary cutters and
craft punches*

IKEA North America Service Inc
496 West Germantown Pike
Plymouth Common
Plymouth Meeting
Philadelphia
PA 19462
tel: (610) 834 0180
www.ikea.com
glassware and mirrors

Michaels
850 North Lade Drive
Suite 500
Coppell
Texas 75019
tel: 1-800 642 4235
email: custhelp@michaels.com
www.michaels.com
general craft supplies

Rainbow Glass
For Rainbow Glass in the United States –
tel: (011 44) 161 790 3025
www.rainbowglass.com

Staedtler Inc
21900 Plummer Street
Catsworth
CA91311
tel: (818) 882 6000
www.custserv@staedtler-usa.com
metal leaf

index

THE AUTHORS

© Matthew Dickens/OnEdition

Alan Gear and **Barry Freestone** are recognized as expert glass painters worldwide. Alan and Barry are also the founders and owners of Rainbow Glass, for which they developed many innovative and exciting glass-painting products that revolutionized the craft for glass painters of all abilities and interests.

Alan came to glass painting via a rather unconventional path, having first trained as an actor and worked in television, film and theatre. When working in the theatre he spent much of his time between scenes painting glass in his dressing room.

Alan and Barry have their own regular show on national UK television, and have made numerous television appearances in Britain, the US and Canada.

Art Nouveau Glass Painting is Alan and Barry's fifth book, but their first for David & Charles. They are based in Manchester, UK.